COURAGE
UNDER FIRE

U.S. NAVY TRUE STORIES

TALES OF BRAVERY

BY JESSICA GUNDERSON

CAPSTONE PRESS
a capstone imprint

Edge Books are published by Capstone Press,
1710 Roe Crest Drive, North Mankato, Minnesota 56003
www.capstonepub.com

Library of Congress Cataloging-in-Publication Data
Gunderson, Jessica.
  U.S. Navy true stories : tales of bravery / by Jessica Gunderson.
    pages cm—(Edge books. Courage under fire)
  Includes bibliographical references and index.
  Summary: "Provides gripping accounts of Navy servicemen and servicewomen who showed
exceptional courage during combat"—Provided by publisher.
  ISBN 978-1-4765-9937-3 (library binding)
  ISBN 978-1-4765-9942-7 (eBook PDF)
1. United States. Navy—Juvenile literature. 2. Sailors—United States—Juvenile literature.
3. Courage—Juvenile literature. I. Title.
  VA58.4.G87 2015
  359.0092′273—dc23   2014004424

Editorial Credits
Christopher L. Harbo, editor; Veronica Scott, designer; Gene Bentdahl, production specialist

Photo Credits
Corbis, 14, 17, Bettmann, 18; Getty Images: AFP/Mehdi Fedouach, 26, Mark Wilson, 20,
Museum of Science and Industry, Chicago, 16, Oleg Nikishin, 23, Pool Photo, 25, U.S. Navy,
15; iStockphotos: lauradyoung, 5 (SS); NARA: U.S. Navy, Office of Public Relations, 12;
Newscom: Fort-Worth Star-Telegram/Paul Moseley, 27; Shutterstock: Jim Barber, 5 (DSC),
R Carner, 5 (BS, PH); U.S. Army, 24; U.S. Naval Historical Center Photograph, 6, 7, 9, 10;
U.S. Navy Photo, cover, 3,17, 20, 28, MC3 David Smart, 29, MCC Gary A. Prill, cover (inset);
Wikimedia: DoD photo, 5 (MOH, NC, NMCCM) 11, (MOH), miscellaneous, 8

Design Elements
Shutterstock: Filipchuk Oleg Vasiliovich, locote, Oleg Zabielin, Petr Vaclavek

Direct Quotations
Page 7 from *The Monitor Boys: The Crew of the Union's First Ironclad* by John V. Quarstein
    (Charleston, S.C.: The History Press, 2011).
Page 8 from *Reign of Iron: The Story of the First Battling Ironclads, the Monitor and the
    Merrimack* by James L. Nelson (New York: HarperCollins, 2004).
Page 14 from "Cook Third Class Doris Miller, USN" Naval History & Heritage Command
    (www.history.navy.mil/faqs/faq57-4.htm).

Printed in the United States of America in Stevens Point, Wisconsin
032014   008092WZF14

TABLE OF CONTENTS

NOT SELF BUT COUNTRY

Throughout history a country's might has often been measured by its navy's strength. Serving at sea, in the air, and on land, the U.S. Navy is the most powerful naval force in the world. Its mission is to be a "global force for good." The Navy's goal is to prevent conflicts, win wars, and maintain freedom of the seas.

The Navy's history stretches all the way back to the Revolutionary War (1775–1783). At that time the Continental Congress voted to send two armed ships to sea to stop the British Navy. Called the Continental Navy, the growing **fleet** helped win American independence. Since that time the Navy has fought in every U.S. war. During World War II (1939–1945), the Navy helped defeat the Japanese in the Pacific. In the Vietnam War (1959–1975), the Navy formed special operations teams called SEALs. These teams carried out dangerous, secret missions, and still do today.

The Navy doesn't have an official **motto**. But its sailors uphold the idea of "not self but country." They answer any call for combat support, rescue help, and disaster relief. Their bravery, selflessness, and honor is at the heart of the U.S. Navy.

fleet—a group of warships under one command
motto—a short statement that tells what a person or organization believes in or stands for

MILITARY AWARDS

Medal of Honor: the highest award for bravery in the U.S. military

Bronze Star: the fourth-highest award for bravery in the U.S. military

Distinguished Service Cross: the second-highest military award for bravery that is given to members of the U.S. Army (and Air Force prior to 1960)

Purple Heart: an award given to members of the military wounded by the enemy in combat

Navy and Marine Corps Commendation Medal: an award given to members of the Navy and Marines for sustained acts of heroism and meritorious service

Navy Cross: the second-highest military award for bravery that is given to members of the Navy and Marines

Silver Star: the third-highest award for bravery in the U.S. military

THE CIVIL WAR

Dates: 1861–1865

The Combatants: Union (Northern states) vs. Confederate States of America (Southern states)

The Victor: Union

Casualties: Union–364,511 dead; Confederate–164,821 dead

The USS *Monitor* (front) and the CSS *Virginia* fire on each other during the Battle of Hampton Roads in 1862.

LIEUTENANT JOHN WORDEN

In March 1862 Union Lieutenant John Lorimer Worden sailed the **ironclad** USS *Monitor* to Hampton Roads, Virginia. He arrived to find the Confederate ironclad *Virginia* attacking the Union warship *Minnesota*.

Worden moved the *Monitor* between the two ships. The two ironclads pounded each other with shells. As Worden raced between the deck and the **pilothouse**, he ordered his crew to keep firing.

During the battle Worden peered between the pilothouse bars when a shell exploded. Metal fragments spun through the air. Worden toppled backward, screaming, "My eyes! I am blind!" Despite his pain, he ordered his **helmsman** to steer away from the *Virginia*.

The crew helped Worden to his cabin. As a doctor plucked iron shards from his eyes, Worden placed Lieutenant Samuel Greene in charge of the *Monitor*. He told Greene, "I cannot see, but don't mind me. Save the *Minnesota* if you can."

The *Monitor* protected the *Minnesota* from further damage, and the *Virginia* left the battle. Worden recovered his eyesight and received the rank of commander. Since then the Navy has named several ships after him.

ironclad—a warship protected by iron or steel plates
pilothouse—the room on a ship with the steering wheel
helmsman—a person who steers a ship

LIEUTENANT ROBERT MINOR

During the Battle of Hampton Roads, the Union warship *Congress* **surrendered** to the Confederates. But the Union ship still sat in the water. Onboard the Confederate ship *Virginia*, Lieutenant Robert Dabney Minor heard his captain say the *Congress* must be burned. He didn't want the Northerners to retake the damaged ship.

Minor immediately offered to lead a small group to burn the ship. He and several other sailors set off for the *Congress* in a small gunboat. As they neared the ship, a hail of gunfire broke out from shore. "The way the balls danced around my little boat and crew was lively beyond measure," Minor recalled. Through the shower of bullets, Minor urged his men on. Suddenly, pain ripped through him. A bullet had pierced his chest and he dropped to the bottom of the boat.

With their leader down, Minor's crew panicked. Despite his bleeding chest, Minor pulled himself to his feet. He calmed the men until a Confederate ship came to their aid.

surrender—to give up or admit defeat in battle

The USS *Congress* (right) sails near Naples, Italy, prior to its involvement in the U.S. Civil War.

Meanwhile the *Virginia* drew close to the *Congress* and set it on fire. Minor recovered and later served as flag lieutenant of the James River Squadron. This squadron was one of the Confederacy's eight major naval forces.

WORLD WAR I

DATES: 1914–1918

THE COMBATANTS: ALLIES (MAIN COUNTRIES: GREAT BRITAIN, FRANCE, ITALY, RUSSIA, UNITED STATES) VS. CENTRAL POWERS (MAIN COUNTRIES: GERMANY, AUSTRIA-HUNGARY, BULGARIA, OTTOMAN EMPIRE)

THE VICTOR: ALLIES

CASUALTIES: ALLIES—5,142,631 DEAD; CENTRAL POWERS—3,386,200 DEAD

Lieutenant Joel T. Boone (second from right) stands with fellow servicemen during World War I.

LIEUTENANT JOEL BOONE

The Navy Medical Corps often serves with Army and Marine units. Although not in direct combat, Medical Corps members often risk their lives to tend the wounded. During World War I, Corps member Lieutenant Joel Thompson Boone did just that.

In July 1918, near Vierzy, France, American and French forces clashed with the German army. As a Navy surgeon, Boone was attached to the 6th Marine **Regiment**. While his group moved into an open field, heavy **artillery** and gunfire bombarded it. Marines fell by the dozen. Through the gunfire, Boone dashed onto the battlefield, medical supplies in tow. Despite explosions and whizzing bullets, he worked furiously to save wounded soldiers.

When Boone's medical supplies ran low, he ran across the battlefield for more. Shells filled with poisonous gas exploded nearby, but Boone kept going. After gathering more supplies, he returned to the battlefield. When his supplies ran low again, he repeated the dangerous trip. American casualties were heavy, but Boone saved many lives.

For his heroism Boone received the Medal of Honor. He went on to serve in World War II and the Korean War (1950–1953). He became the nation's most decorated medical officer. He earned the Army's Distinguished Service Cross, a Silver Star, and many other honors.

regiment—a large group of soldiers who fight together as a unit
artillery—cannons and other large guns used during battles

WORLD WAR II

DATES: 1939–1945

THE COMBATANTS: ALLIES (MAIN COUNTRIES: GREAT BRITAIN, FRANCE, RUSSIA, UNITED STATES) VS. AXIS POWERS (MAIN COUNTRIES: GERMANY, ITALY, JAPAN)

THE VICTOR: ALLIES

CASUALTIES: ALLIES—14,141,544 DEAD; AXIS—5,634,232 DEAD

Billowing plumes of smoke rise from the USS *West Virginia* during the attack on Pearl Harbor on December 7, 1941.

MESS ATTENDANT SECOND CLASS DORIS MILLER

In 1939 Doris "Dorie" Miller joined the U.S. Navy as a **mess attendant**. This position was one of only a few open to African-Americans at that time. By 1941 he was assigned to the USS *West Virginia*, stationed in Pearl Harbor, Hawaii.

On the morning of December 7, 1941, Miller was collecting laundry when the ship's alarm blared. He raced to the upper deck. Overhead nearly 200 Japanese fighter planes circled the sky. They rained bombs down on the *West Virginia* and the other U.S. battleships. Pearl Harbor was under attack.

Miller rushed through the smoke. Because of his large size and strength, he was ordered to help move the wounded away from the burning upper deck. Suddenly, a lieutenant called him to help the ship's injured captain. With two others, Miller carried the captain away from the smoke and deck fires.

mess attendant—a person who cooks and cleans for officers on a ship

The lieutenant then ordered Miller to man an antiaircraft machine gun. Without any training on the weapon, Miller began firing at the planes. "It wasn't hard," he recalled. "I just pulled the trigger and she worked fine. I had watched the others with these guns."

Doris "Dorie" Miller

The Japanese planes zoomed close, and Miller continued to fire. For fifteen minutes he pounded ammunition into the sky. Bombs soared above him, oily fires sprang up on the deck, and thick smoke swirled about the ship. Water whooshed across the deck as sailors rushed to put out the fires. Despite the chaos, Miller kept to his post until he ran out of ammunition. Soon he heard the call to abandon the sinking *West Virginia*.

Of the 1,541 sailors onboard the *West Virginia*, 130 were killed and 52 were wounded. For his brave actions, Miller became the first African-American to receive the Navy Cross. He also received the Purple Heart. He died in 1943 while onboard the aircraft carrier *Liscome Bay* that was under attack from a Japanese submarine. In June 1973 the USS *Miller* was named in his honor.

USS *West Virginia*

LIEUTENANT ALBERT DAVID

During World War II, the Atlantic Ocean swarmed with German U-boat submarines. On June 4, 1944, a group of U.S. warships located Germany's *U-505*. By pounding the water with **depth charges**, they forced the sub to the surface. As Germans leaped from the U-boat, Lieutenant Albert Leroy David sprung into action. He and a team of sailors from the USS *Pillsbury* scrambled onto a small motorboat. They sped toward the sub and jumped to its slippery deck. David knew Germans could be hiding below or the sub could explode or sink at any moment. But despite the risks, he plunged down the submarine's hatch.

The sub was empty but sinking fast. Swells of water broke across the deck and whooshed down the hatch. David called to the men on deck to close the hatch. Then he raced toward the radio room to retrieve the enemy's secret codes and charts.

depth charge—a metal can filled with explosives

As David and his men prowled the belly of the sub, another group arrived to help keep it afloat. *U-505* was the Navy's first captured enemy vessel at sea since 1815. For his brave actions, David was awarded the Medal of Honor.

The USS *Pillsbury* sits alongside the German submarine *U-505* after it was captured on June 4, 1944.

U.S. sailors stand on the deck of *U-505* shortly after capturing it.

THE VIETNAM WAR

DATES: 1959–1975

THE COMBATANTS: UNITED STATES, SOUTH VIETNAM, AND THEIR ALLIES VS. NORTH VIETNAM AND ITS ALLIES

THE VICTOR: NORTH VIETNAM

CASUALTIES: UNITED STATES–58,220 DEAD; SOUTH VIETNAM–ESTIMATED 200,000 TO 250,000 DEAD; NORTH VIETNAM–ESTIMATED 1.1 MILLION DEAD

Navy SEALs watch an explosion destroy an enemy bunker in Vietnam.

PETTY OFFICER MICHAEL THORNTON

In October 1972 Petty Officer Michael E. Thornton was part of a Navy SEAL team on a secret mission behind enemy lines. Its goal was to cut off the North Vietnamese Army's (NVA) supply route.

As the team moved inland from the seashore, the enemy peppered them with gunfire. Then a grenade landed near Thornton. He tossed it between himself and the enemy several times before it exploded nearby. **Shrapnel** raked his back, but he was able to regroup with his team behind a sand dune. When Thornton got there, he was told team member Thomas Norris had been shot dead.

Thornton didn't hesitate. He raced to Norris' body, lifted it over his shoulders, and ran. The NVA chased at full speed, shooting wildly. An explosion knocked Thornton to the ground, and he lost his grip on Norris' body. As Thornton crawled toward him, he heard a voice say his name. To his surprise, Norris was still alive!

Thornton grabbed Norris again and rushed into the water. He put his life jacket on Norris, strapped him to his back, and swam with all his might. After hours of swimming, a U.S. boat finally rescued them. Thomas Norris survived his wounds. Michael Thornton received the Medal of Honor for risking his life to save his teammate.

shrapnel—pieces that have broken off something after an explosion

OPERATION ENDURING FREEDOM

DATES: 2001–PRESENT

THE COMBATANTS: AFGHANISTAN GOVERNMENT, THE UNITED STATES AND ITS COALITION FORCES VS. AL-QAIDA **TERRORIST** ORGANIZATION AND THE TALIBAN, AN ISLAMIC GROUP THAT SUPPORTS AL-QAIDA

THE VICTOR: CONFLICT ONGOING

CASUALTIES: AMERICAN AND COALITION FORCES (THROUGH DECEMBER 6, 2012)–3,215 DEAD; AFGHAN CIVILIANS (REPORTED FROM JANUARY 2007 TO JUNE 2012)–13,009 DEAD; TALIBAN AND AL-QAIDA–NUMBER UNKNOWN

Lieutenant Michael Murphy

Maureen Murphy holds the Medal of Honor awarded to her husband, Michael, after his death in Afghanistan.

LIEUTENANT MICHAEL MURPHY

On June 27, 2005, a helicopter dropped Lieutenant Michael Murphy, and three other Navy SEALs, into a mountainous region in Afghanistan. Their mission was to find the hideout of Mullah Ahmad Shah. He led a terrorist group called the Mountain Tigers.

As Murphy scanned the mountainside with binoculars, he saw 30 to 40 armed Taliban fighters pointing rifles in their direction. The SEALs were trapped. Gunfire rang out as the enemy closed in. The SEALs bounded down the mountain, shooting back at the Taliban fighters. A bullet smashed into Murphy's stomach, but he continued to fight. He called to his team to keep moving.

After an hour of fighting, one SEAL was dead and the rest severely injured. Murphy tried to radio for help but he couldn't get through. He knew he needed to find a signal to save his men. He ran out into open ground, in plain sight of the enemy. Pelted with bullets, he managed to contact headquarters before a shot pierced his back, killing him.

Murphy's brave actions led to the rescue of his last surviving teammate, Marcus Luttrell. Murphy **posthumously** received the Medal of Honor for his actions. He was also awarded the Silver Star and the Purple Heart.

terrorist—a person who uses violence to kill, injure, or make people and governments afraid

posthumous—coming or happening after death

CHIEF PETTY OFFICER STEPHEN BASS

In November 2001 Taliban prisoners overtook a fortress near Mazar-e-Sharif, Afghanistan. Chief Petty Officer Stephen Bass, a Navy SEAL, joined an American and British rescue team to recover two Americans trapped inside. One was believed to be injured and possibly even dead.

Under a rain of bullets and the thunder of grenades, Bass quickly made his way into the fortress. He reached an active minefield and, despite the danger, crossed it to reach the heart of the fortress. When he saw that one American was alive, Bass dropped down and crawled toward him. But the enemy fire was too dangerous. It forced Bass to turn back.

Bass reported the location of the uninjured American. The team made a plan to rescue him. But they made no plans to recover the other American, believing him dead. Bass couldn't leave without knowing for sure if the man was dead. As night fell he went back inside alone. Enemy gunfire greeted him, but he continued forward, firing back.

When he ran out of ammunition, he grabbed weapons from the bodies of Taliban fighters and used them to fight back. At last he reached the second American. Only when he knew for sure that the American was dead, did he retreat from the fortress. For his courageous attempts to rescue the trapped Americans, Bass received a Navy Cross.

U.S. soldiers take cover during an explosion prior to battling Taliban forces in a fortress near Mazar-e-Sharif, Afghanistan, in November 2001.

SENIOR CHIEF PETTY OFFICER BRITT SLABINSKI

In March 2002 Senior Chief Petty Officer Britt Slabinski led a team of SEALs to rescue a teammate from enemy territory in the Afghan mountains. When the SEALs jumped from the helicopter, blasts of gunfire surrounded them. The snow-covered Takur Ghar mountaintop crawled with enemy forces. Slabinski and the SEALs fired back, killing several enemy fighters. During the fighting Slabinski alerted air support to the enemy's position on the mountaintop.

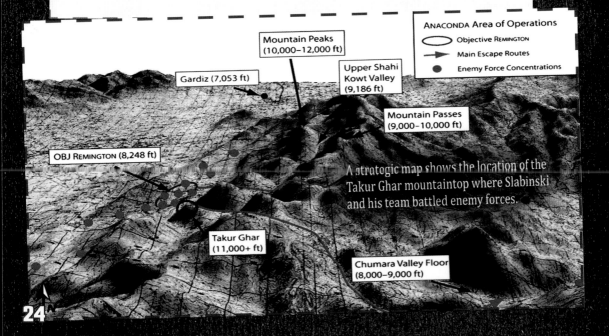

Mountain Peaks
(10,000–12,000 ft)

Gardiz (7,053 ft)

Upper Shahi
Kowt Valley
(9,186 ft)

ANACONDA Area of Operations

⬭ Objective REMINGTON

➤ Main Escape Routes

● Enemy Force Concentrations

Mountain Passes
(9,000–10,000 ft)

OBJ REMINGTON (8,248 ft)

A strategic map shows the location of the Takur Ghar mountaintop where Slabinski and his team battled enemy forces.

Takur Ghar
(11,000+ ft)

Chumara Valley Floor
(8,000–9,000 ft)

A CH-47 Chinook helicopter lands in the Afghan mountains in March 2002.

In the gunfight two SEALs were wounded, and Slabinski knew they could not continue the rescue mission. He hoisted one wounded man into his arms and trekked down the mountain, dodging enemy bullets. Through waist-high snow and bitter cold, he and his team carried the wounded SEALs until a rescue helicopter came to their aid.

Both injured SEALs survived. Slabinski received a Navy Cross for alerting forces to the enemy's position and saving his wounded men.

OPERATION IRAQI FREEDOM

DATES: 2003–2011

THE COMBATANTS: THE UNITED STATES AND COALITION FORCES VS. IRAQ, FIRST THE GOVERNMENT OF SADDAM HUSSEIN AND THEN **INSURGENTS**

THE VICTOR: THE UNITED STATES DEFEATED SADDAM HUSSEIN IN 2003 BUT THEN FACED STIFF FIGHTING FROM INSURGENTS UNTIL ITS WITHDRAWAL IN 2011

CASUALTIES: AMERICAN AND COALITION FORCES—4,804 DEAD; IRAQI SOLDIERS AND INSURGENTS—ESTIMATED MORE THAN 30,000 DEAD

U.S. Marines patrol a street in Fallujah, Iraq, in 2004.

insurgent—a person who rebels and fights against his or her country's ruling government and those supporting it

SEAL TEAM 3 CHIEF CHRIS KYLE

During Operation Iraqi Freedom, Navy SEAL Chris Kyle became the deadliest **sniper** in U.S. history. His courage matched his sniper skills in Fallujah, Iraq, in 2004. One day while perched on a rooftop, he eyed the streets for enemy activity. As he peered through his gun's scope, the sound of gunfire filled the air.

Kyle left his position and sprinted down the street. He found a group of Marines who told him the insurgents had trapped some of their men. Kyle raced in their direction. Insurgents fired at him, and he fired back. When he rounded a corner, he spotted four soldiers huddled near a wall. He told them to run while he covered them. As the men fled, Kyle noticed a Marine sprawled on the ground. The soldier had been shot in both legs. Kyle grabbed him by his body armor and dragged him as he dashed for safety.

As he fled, a grenade explosion knocked pieces of wall onto Kyle and injured his leg. But he kept running until he and the injured Marine reached shelter. Kyle was awarded a Bronze Star for his bravery in combat. He went on to receive several more Bronze and Silver Stars for his courageous service.

sniper—a soldier trained to shoot at long-distance targets from a hidden place

COMMANDER LENORA LANGLAIS

In 2006 Commander Lenora Langlais arrived in Iraq as part of the Navy Medical Corps. On April 7 she was walking at the airbase when enemy bombs dropped from the sky. Sand swirled into the air from the explosions. As Langlais ran for cover, a bomb burst directly above her. Chunks of shrapnel slammed into her neck and face. She dropped to the ground, blood streaming from her neck. A medical team rushed her to the trauma center and quickly operated.

After the operation Langlais refused to go to another hospital for better care. As the most experienced nurse on the airbase, she knew her help was needed. Despite her injuries she helped a patient who was having an allergic reaction to medication. Langlais received a Purple Heart for her service.

Langlais speaks with high school students at a Navy training program in 2009.

On land and at sea, Navy sailors risk their lives to defend the United States. They serve with pride and never give a second thought to putting themselves in harm's way. Their stories are more than just exciting tales from the battlefield. They display the strength of our fighting men and women and their incredible courage under fire.

artillery (ar-TI-luhr-ee)—cannons and other large guns used during battles

casualty (KAZH-oo-uhl-tee)—someone who is injured, captured, killed, or missing in an accident, a disaster, or a war

depth charge (DEPTH CHAHRJ)—a metal can filled with explosives

fleet (FLEET)—a group of warships under one command

helmsman (HELMZ-muhn)—a person who steers a ship

insurgent (in-SUR-juhnt)—a person who rebels and fights against his or her country's ruling government and those supporting it

ironclad (EYE-urn-klad)—a warship protected by iron or steel plates

mess attendant (MESS uh-TEN-duhnt)—a person who cooks and cleans for officers on a ship

motto (MOT-oh)—a short statement that tells what a person or organization believes in or stands for

pilothouse (PYE-luht HOUSS)—the room on a ship with the steering wheel

posthumous (POHST-huh-muhss)—coming or happening after death

regiment (REJ-uh-muhnt)—a large group of soldiers who fight together as a unit

shrapnel (SHRAP-nuhl)—pieces that have broken off something after an explosion

sniper (SNY-pur)—a soldier trained to shoot at long-distance targets from a hidden place

surrender (suh-REN-dur)—to give up or admit defeat in battle

terrorist (TER-ur-ist)—a person who uses violence to kill, injure, or make people and governments afraid

READ MORE

Goldish, Meish. *Navy: Civilian to Sailor.* Becoming a Soldier. New York: Bearport Publishing, 2011.

Harasymiw, Mark. *Heroes of the U.S. Navy.* Heroes of the U.S. Military. New York: Gareth Stevens Publishing, 2013.

Rudolph, Jessica. *Today's Navy Heroes.* Acts of Courage: Inside America's Military. New York: Bearport Publishing, 2012.

SELECT BIBLIOGRAPHY

Dockery, Kevin. *Navy Seals: A History Part II—The Vietnam Years.* New York: Berkley Books, 2002.

Holmstedt, Kirsten. *The Girls Come Marching Home: Stories of Women Warriors Returning from the War in Iraq.* Mechanicsburg, Pa.: Stackpole Books, 2009.

Kyle, Chris. *American Sniper: The Autobiography of the Most Lethal Sniper in U.S. Military History.* New York: William Morrow, 2012.

Martin, Iain C. The Greatest U.S. Navy Stories Ever Told. Guilford, Conn.: The Lyons Press, 2006.

Nelson, James L. *Reign of Iron: The Story of the First Battling Ironclads, the Monitor and the Merrimack.* New York: William Morrow, 2004.

Quarstein, John V. *The Monitor Boys: The Crew of the Union's First Ironclad.* Charleston, S.C.: The History Press, 2011.

Williams, Gary. *Seal of Honor: Operation Red Wings and the Life of Lt. Michael P. Murphy, USN.* Annapolis, Md.: Naval Institute Press, 2010.

FactHound offers a safe, fun way to find Internet sites related to this book. All of the sites on FactHound have been researched by our staff.

Here's all you do:

Visit www.facthound.com

Type in this code: 9781476599373

Check out projects, games and lots more at
www.capstonekids.com

INDEX